Prison Segmentation for Sound Healing Drug Alternatives

Homeostasis Tools

Reverend Mike Wanner

Copyright
Rev. Mike Wanner, May 13, 2018

Selected Images Used by License

Table of Contents

Copyright 2
Table of Contents 3
Introduction 4
Acknowledgments 5
1 - Why I am Writing This Book 7
2 - The Natural Order of Healing 8
3 - Sound Healing Supports Homeostasis 9
4 - About Sound Healing 10
5 - Drumming 11
6 - Classical Music Traditional Soothing 12
7 - Folk Music 13
8 - Silence Can Soothe 14
9 - Addiction Healing Sound Goals 15
10 - Ideas to Consider 16
11 - Sound Healing Tools 19
12 - The Goal 20
13 - Healing is Optimized When Chakra Energy Centers Are Balanced . 21
14 - Chakra Characteristics 22
15 - The Journey of Healing 23
16 - God is Your Light 25
17 - Thank You 26
18 - Don't Worry Ever 27
19 - Book Resource Categories 28
20 - Angels Please Prayers 29
21 - Prison Presents Project 30
22 - Private Channeling 31
23 - Reverend Mike Wanner 32

Introduction

I have published 52 books so far about prison possibilities, and the complexity of the issues continues to boggle my mind. Steps in the right direction are easy for me to conceive but creating a plan means I need to establish justification for the effort.

The noise of prison may seem deafening to observers. One only needs to go to YouTube to see videos where the noise level is extreme and disturbing to the listener.

In my head, I think of the phrase - music soothes the savage beast, so I set out to find the origins and went to ask.com.

The answer I found was -
"What is the origin of 'Music soothes the savage beast'?
Answer by CD Lady

The actual phrase in modern English is:
"Music has Charms to soothe a savage Breast"

The phrase was coined by the Playwright/Poet William Congreve, in The Mourning Bride."

Acknowledgments

I would like to acknowledge the following Beautiful, Charming, Delightful Human Beings for their Spiritual Significance and Service.

Sharon Kachel - Sound Healer

Sharon Kachel - Attuned by Spirit on Facebook.com

Bliss through Sound Healing, Meditation, and Reiki.

Website - http://www.attunedwithspirit.com/

Debbra Lupien - The Answer Diva

Debbra Lupien, The Answer Diva on Facebook.com

Author of Akasha Unleashed; The Missing Manual to You

Debbra's Program Rock Your Life 2018 rocked mine.

Website - http://akashaunleashed.com/

The Akashic Records Made No Sense to me before
I Met Debbra. She breaks it down for everybody.

1 - Why I am Writing This Book

Prisons have many problems, and the most troublesome pair is likely mental crises and addiction. I would never criticize efforts to help the afflicted, but from what I read, it seems more help is needed.

It seems logical to me that we need to soften the intensity of noise in prison as it may be deafening to the minds that need healing.

I have written a lot about segmenting prisons in the hope of adding security as a foundation for better peace of mind. Using segmentation to find quiet could be foundational to a level of peace and tranquility that can lead to the potential for healing.

The right music could further that effort and help residents step down their stress and step up their healing. Segmentation for anything could include some options that bring soothing music to the residents to diminish their guardedness and prepare them for positive outcomes.

Like Muzak on elevators and in stores has been used in times past to help quiet the minds for customers during their user experience, creative thinking could be used in prisons to lessen the level of stress, anxiety, and unrest.

Like a relief valve on a pressurized system, avoidance of explosions can be a significant goal.

2 - The Natural Order of Healing

Homeostasis

Dictionary.com defines Homeostasis as "the tendency of a system, especially the physiological system of higher animals, to maintain internal stability, owing to the coordinated response of its parts to any situation or stimulus that would tend to disturb its normal condition or function.

3 - Sound Healing Supports Homeostasis

Providing prisoners with available, legal and appropriate options to their addiction patterns could go a long way to Change the situation for all concerned,

Music could be a no-brainer if this was of interest to prison program directors. Music selection can create issues within the community as the variety and intensity of musical interests is very diverse.

Age and upbringing can have a lot to do with perceptions about music. Segmentation, however, provides a controlled environment where the benefits could be reaped without dissenter complications.

The simple idea of being able to mellow out to a comfortable mindset of choice could go a long way to claim a bit of mental freedom and peace of mind.

Different groups with a segment could keep things rocking in a positive way.

Of course, the administration would need to have an oversight level that chooses options to be available that are appropriate with little likelihood of problematic reactions.

4 - About Sound Healing

Sound Healing can be more like a healing science than musical entertainment so as to customize the frequencies for the needs of the listeners.

Ideally, the day will come, where a clinical prescription for support of prisoners could be written to provide for a subtle economical ongoing healing progression through sound healing that both a clinician and a user can mutually agree upon.

Just to be clear, there is no suggestion here of subconscious interference with the free will of users but on the other hand, only a deliberate option to openly offer choices that benefit the user and the common good of the community.

It can be helpful to target slices of the community with precise complaints so that sound support of precisely targeted efforts is a more common use than an applied general broadcast that diffuses too broadly, so results are unimpressive.

5 - Drumming

Native Americans used drumming for vibrational entrainment to ground themselves and prepare for spiritual enlightenment.

6 - Classical Music Traditional Soothing

The Classical Musicians of the finest Orchestras have soothed the stresses of many nations for centuries.

7 - Folk Music

The Music of the people can help make people feel hopeful and relaxed which is a starting point for many things which can benefit many people. Folk Music can make people feel at home.

Our prisons are very diverse, and segmentation can allow an optimal number of people to find optimism and a bit of peace. From optimism can come creativity and change.

8 - Silence Can Soothe

9 - Addiction Healing Sound Goals

Even with a bit of peace and soothing, it may not be enough for those who have been addicted, but that should not stop the effort. One step at a time is an old perspective builder.

Highs and lows in life pass eventually, the sting of the present is part of the motivation for those with addiction habits. The problem with addiction is that which is used to soothe the pain evolves into an expansiveness of the problem.

The goal would be to find acceptable legal substitutes for the addiction substance of choice that can be used without contraindicated complications. Drumming can help, and music can help, but there can also be sound tools which go further.

What would it be like if a prisoner who was Jones-ing for a fix could call a guard and request a sound healing treatment/experience that could mellow them out, soften the stress focus and leave them relieved somewhat and rejuvenated a bit without a residual depressive physical reaction or remorse?

It would be problem resolution without complications and/or consequences. Pretty Good That.

10 - Ideas to Consider

1. Appropriateness.
   Music or treatment selected should be appropriate to the individual and all they need to work on.

2. Sound Healing Sequencing.
   As vibratory dynamics are experienced, it would be most useful if a progression of selection upgrades allows a subtle, consistent raising of the vibrations and results.

3. Delivery methods
   Variation of delivery devices can lead to subtle upgrades so all successes could be documented so as to provide justification for additional later expenses.

4. Mental Preparation
   Planning can enhance success, so it is essential that planning prep is accomplished.

5. Avoid jumping about without evaluation
   There can be a tendency to jump from thing to thing to something, but that is not recommended as that promotes disconnection instead of success. It is essential to know for sure what does and does not work.

6. Foreground more often that Background.
   Consciousness interacts heavily with results. Background works but active listening can raise awareness and success.

7. Pay attention to the music, words, and meaning.
   The total experience matters so let us consider all parts as essential elements to manifest.

8. Enjoy the whole experience before evaluation.
   If you take the necessary time to do the experience, and then the time required to do the evaluation, then you will have both in a way that can be an excellent resource.

9. Response and reactions within.
   Shifts going on within are very important, please pay attention to them.

10. Active participation in Physical Healing

11. Active participation in Emotional Healing

12. Active participation in Mental Healing

13. Active participation in Spiritual Healing

14. Silence after Sound Healing to maximize absorption!

15. Experience Journals Analysis

16. What is needed next?

17. Problems to be solved in journals.

18. Symptom lists with applied results.

11 - Sound Healing Tools

Chants
Healing pipes
Singing Bowls
Tuning Forks
White Noise
CD's
DVDs
Chakra Clearing and Healing sounds
Tingshas
Programmed Crystals
Crystal Music
Gongs
Drums
Programmed Meditations
Chimes
Marimba
Musical Instruments of all kinds
Bells
Crystals

12 - The Goal

The

Goal

of

Sound Healing

is

Nurture of the Chakras

To Optimize

Homeostasis

and

Healing

13 - Healing is Optimized When Chakra Energy Centers Are Balanced

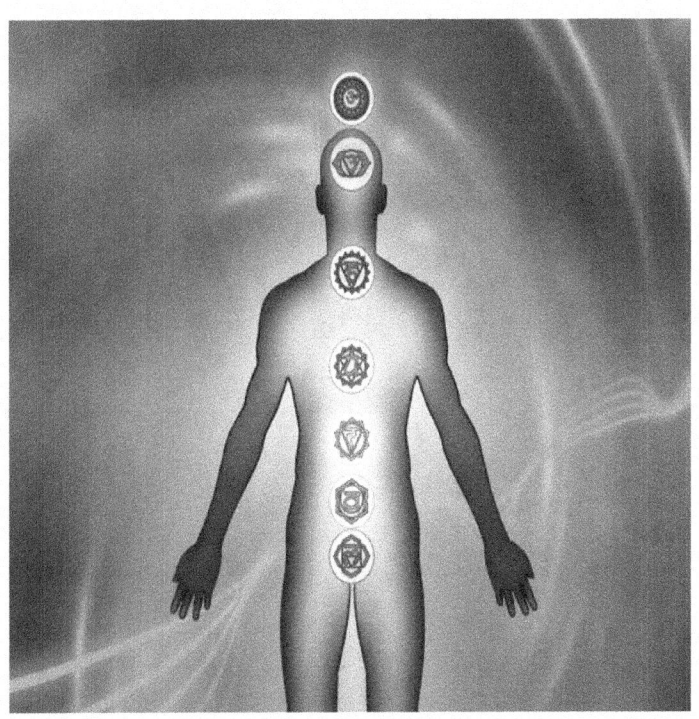

14 - Chakra Characteristics

{Chakra Overview from Chapter 8 - Antennae To God: 777 Book Zero}

Seven Energy Centers (Chakras) of the Energy Body

From the Highest To The Lowest

#	Name	Locations	Color	Musical Note	Gland
7	Crown	Top/Head	Violet/White	B	Pineal
6	3Rd Eye	Forehead	Indigo	A	Pituitary
5	Throat	Throat	Blue	G	Thyroid
4	Heart	Center/Chest	Green/Pink	F	Thymus
3	Solar Plexus	Solar Plexus	Yellow	E	Pancreas
2	Sacral	Spleen	Orange	D	Gonads
1	Root	Tailbone	Red	C	Adrenals

15 - The Journey of Healing

The Journey of Healing can be difficult for us mortals, and it can be even more complicated when the information that we are able to find comes from conflicting sources. We can get very caught up in trying to find the right information and stress about it to such a degree that we begin to work against ourselves.

Guidance is available, but we can only find it when we know we are in touch with the right sources. Sound can help us, humans, balance. Prayer and meditation are resources to consider when we seek guidance.

Meditation which is a fantastic resource can seem more difficult than it is. I, myself, had some trouble with both prayer and meditation as I have a tendency to take everything quite literally, and initially, I did not relax into the subtly of them and thought I was doing them wrong.

Persistence will serve you well as will gratitude and ease. As a young man, I was angry as I lost my father at an early age and felt a massive unfairness in my struggle.

I learned, and I hope all do who persist, are patient, and have gratitude. Prayer works better than ever for me because I endured.

A Meditative state works within my writing as my persistence in answer seeking has caused me to learn a lot and write a lot, and in the process, I am reflectively absorbing harmony with all that is.

I wish every reader patience and a belief in your ability to connect with higher vibrations. The Divine can help it to manifest. Sound healing can also help you find your peace and vibrate higher.

Finding your balance in the way that is perfect and right for you is optimal for healing. The peaks and valleys of existence can modulate over time when you have invited balance and accepted the reality that many things will eventually be better for yourself and all who you care about.

At one time I overthought and learned too little. I recommend thinking less, being peaceful, appreciating the beauty of nature surrounding us and then offering thanks.

Many people worry, and I do not recommend that because it does not work. What you focus on has a tendency to increase in your life. May you focus only on things you want to attract.

I focus on my blessings, and it seems I always have more. By that I am not talking about money or fancy cars, I am talking about benefits that tickle my heart. I recommend Gratitude.

May God Bless You and May You Bless Yourself.
AND SO IT IS!

16 - God is Your Light

*

Your Goal Can Be to Reconnect With The Light

*

Remember The Clear Light

Remember the clear light,

The pure, clear white light

From which everything in the universe comes,

To which everything in the universe returns;

The original nature of your own mind.

The natural state of the universe unmanifest.

Let go into the clear light, trust it, merge with it.

It is your own true nature; it is home.

(From - The Tibetan Book Of The Dead)

17 - Thank You

For Considering These Ideas

18 - Don't Worry Ever

It Does Not Help Prayer Still Does!

Resource: http://Create-A-Prayer.com

19 - Book Resource Categories

Veterans Healing Six Pack plus 2
http://angelraphaelspeaks.com/healing-books/veterans/

PTSD Power Pack
http://angelraphaelspeaks.com/healing-books/ptsd/

Angel Raphael Speaks Series & Other Angel Books
http://angelraphaelspeaks.com/

Reiki
http://angelraphaelspeaks.com/healing-books/reiki/

Children
http://angelraphaelspeaks.com/healing-books/children/

Emergency Medical Kindness
http://angelraphaelspeaks.com/healing-books/emergency-medical-kindness/

Cancer
http://angelraphaelspeaks.com/healing-books/cancer/

Addictions
http://angelraphaelspeaks.com/healing-books/addictions/

Miscellaneous Healing
http://angelraphaelspeaks.com/healing-books/misc-healing/

Prison Books - 50+ Prison Books
http://angelraphaelspeaks.com/prison-books/

{Distant Healing (or Mail List) e-mail mikewann@voicenet.com}

20 - Angels Please Prayers

Addict's
Angels of Healing Selected
Help Me to Stay Directed
Come To Me From The Sky
I Am Ready to Succeed Not Try
If I Don't Invite You In
I Might Not Win
I Have Been Lost For Too Long
Help Me To Stay Strong

&

Alcoholic's
Angels of Healing On High
Help Me to Stay Dry
Come To Me From The Sky
I Am Ready to Succeed Not Try
If I Don't Invite You In
I Might Not Win
I Have Been Lost For Too Long
Help Me To Stay Strong

From

http://AngelRaphaelSpeaks.com/AAAAAAA/

21 - Prison Presents Project

I am offering my prison books on a rotating basis as Free Kindles on the website
http://angelraphaelspeaks.com/christmas/

Presents for Prisoners, Their Families and You Started Christmas Day 2017

I channel the Angel of Healing – Archangel Raphael who has motivated me to write a lot about healing prisons and saving the American economy from death by prison costs.

I have published 51+ books about prison possibilities alone and offer most of them as presents every five days or so through Kindle to all who would like them. The release schedule is at the website referenced above, and it will be added to as time goes by.

Angel Raphael Speaks – Prisons was a spinoff e-book of the Angel Raphael Channeling, and the Angel Raphael Speaks Series of channeled messages. There were only 14 messages in that book out of the approximately three hundred that came through the series. Those 14 messages and eight that came later spurred an invitation that took me to write the 51+ prison books that I have now published about prisons.

I have no expertise in prisons but listen well to Spirit. I have given away thousands of my healing books to veterans and others. I am an ordained minister through both the Circles of Miracles Ministry in New Britain, PA and the International Metaphysical Ministry in Sedona, AZ. May all who read this be blessed AND SO IT IS!

Reverend Mike Wanner, mikewann@voicenet.com, 215-342-1270

22 - Private Channeling

Angel Raphael Speaks a series of free messages that are channeled through Reverend Mike Wanner for the Highest good and Highest Healing of all concerned.

Many questions arise about Reverend Mike doing private channeling, and he does help with that so E-mail him.

Reverend Mike is available worldwide as a distant healer, psychic channel, emotional release facilitator, spiritual energy practitioner & teacher, and public speaker. He looks forward to meeting you soon!

Email - mikewann@voicenet.com 215-342-1270

PRIVATE SPIRITUAL READINGS/channelings or Spiritual Healing Sessions: Telephone or in person.

Rev. Mike is available for individual, intuitive one-on-one sessions with you, his Guide Family, and your Guides. He helps by offering clarity on emotional situations about your life, your purpose, your spirituality, and your release of stuffed emotions and cellular memory.

Connect to the love of your Guides today!

For more information, Please visit
http://angelraphaelspeaks.com/channel/

23 - Reverend Mike Wanner

Rev. Mike Wanner started his spiritual and ministerial studies with Reiki in 1993 and had studied seven styles of Reiki in the U.S., Japan, Canada, Denmark and Australia. He is certified to teach. He became certified to teach Integrated Energy Therapy in 1999 and co-taught the first IET class of the new Millennium. Mike began dowsing in 2001.

Ordained as an Interfaith Minister of the Circle of Miracles Ministry and a Metaphysical Minister of the International Metaphysical Ministry, Rev. Mike practices and teaches spiritual energy therapies in the Philadelphia Area.

Rev. Mike holds ministerial degrees from the University of Metaphysics and the University of Sedona. He is a Pastoral Care Associate at Jefferson Frankford Hospital. He taught at the National Academy of Massage Therapy and Health Sciences.

Rev. Mike was a faculty member of the Medical Mission Sister's Center for Human Integration's School of Integrated Body/Mind Therapies in Fox Chase, Philadelphia, PA for twelve years.

For a complete Biography, Please visit
http://ReverendMikeWanner.com/Bio

www.ingramcontent.com/pod-product-compliance
Lightning Source LLC
Chambersburg PA
CBHW030040230526
45472CB00002B/604